I0797672

Gross Stuff!

Gross Stuff with Animals

by Julie Murray

Dash!
LEVELED READERS
An Imprint of Abdo Zoom • abdobooks.com

Level 1 – Beginning
Short and simple sentences with familiar words or patterns for children who are beginning to understand how letters and sounds go together.

Level 2 – Emerging
Longer words and sentences with more complex language patterns for readers who are practicing common words and letter sounds.

Level 3 – Transitional
More developed language and vocabulary for readers who are becoming more independent.

abdobooks.com

Published by Abdo Zoom, a division of ABDO, PO Box 398166, Minneapolis, Minnesota 55439.

Printed in the United States of America, North Mankato, Minnesota.
052025
092025

Photo Credits: Alamy, Getty Images, Minden Pictures, Science Source, Shutterstock
Production Contributors: Jennie Forsberg, Grace Hansen, John Hansen
Design Contributors: Candice Keimig, Neil Klinepier

Library of Congress Control Number: 2024947653

Publisher's Cataloging in Publication Data

Names: Murray, Julie, author.
Title: Gross stuff with animals / by Julie Murray
Description: Minneapolis, Minnesota : Abdo Zoom, 2026 | Series: Gross stuff! | Includes online resources and index.
Identifiers: ISBN 9781098288662 (lib. bdg.) | ISBN 9781098289362 (ebook) | ISBN 9781098289713 (Read-to-me ebook)
Subjects: LCSH: Cleanliness--Juvenile literature. | Animal husbandry--Juvenile literature. | Animal pests--Juvenile literature. | Diseases and pests--Juvenile literature. | Sanitation--Juvenile literature. | Curiosities and wonders--Juvenile literature.
Classification: DDC 590--dc23

Table of Contents

Gross Stuff with Animals

While some animals do cute things, others can be just plain gross! But they have very good reasons for their gross behaviors.

Body Functions

Ornate narrow-mouthed frogs live in piles of elephant poop! They do this to stay cool. They also find tasty things to eat.

A male Surinam toad puts **fertilized** eggs on a female's back. The female's skin grows around the eggs. The young frogs are born from their mother's back!

Flies taste with their feet. They land on everything, from dog poop to food. They also vomit and poop every time they land on food!

Turkey vultures poop and pee on their legs. This keeps them cool. They can also shoot their vomit up to 10 feet (3.04 m) to keep **predators** away.

Female desert spiders give their lives for their young. The mother spider **regurgitates** her body fluids to feed her babies. Then, the babies **puncture** her stomach to get more fluids. In the end, only a shell of her is left.

Self Defense

The Texas horned lizard has a gross way to keep **predators** at bay. It can raise the **blood pressure** in its head. This causes the blood vessels around the eyes to shoot blood!

A sea cucumber can eject its **intestines** and other organs. This can distract or trap **predators**. The sea cucumber then regrows the lost body parts within a few weeks.

Hagfish are eel-like animals that live on the ocean floor. When they feel scared, they release lots of slime. This covers **predators** and makes it hard for them to breathe.

More Facts

- The tongue-eating louse feeds on fish tongues. Once the tongue falls off, the louse attaches itself and becomes the fish's new tongue.

- Bombardier beetles spray their **predators** with hot chemicals that are stored in sacs in their bodies. The chemicals can reach 212 °F (100 °C)!

- Hagfish feed on dead fish. They bury themselves in the bodies. Then, they eat their way from the inside out!

Glossary

blood pressure – pressure of the blood on the walls of blood vessels.

fertilize – to make able to produce babies or eggs.

intestine – a long tube made up of the small intestine and large intestine that helps digest food, absorb nutrients and water, and carries waste out of the body.

predator – an animal that hunts other animals for food.

puncture – to make a small hole in something.

regurgitate – to pour back out from a place of containment.

Index

Online Resources

To learn more about gross animal stuff, please visit **abdobooklinks.com** or scan this QR code. These links are routinely monitored and updated to provide the most current information available.